THE UNEXPLAINED

NEAR-DEATH EXPERIENCES

BY ADAM STONE

BELLWETHER MEDIA • MINNEAPOLIS, MN

Are you ready to take it to the extreme?
Torque books thrust you into the action-packed world
of sports, vehicles, mystery, and adventure. These books
may include dirt, smoke, fire, and dangerous stunts.
WARNING: read at your own risk.

Library of Congress Cataloging-in-Publication Data

Stone, Adam.
  Near-death experiences / by Adam Stone.
      p. cm. -- (Torque : the unexplained)
  Summary: "Engaging images accompany information about near-death experiences.
The combination of high-interest subject matter and light text is intended for students in
grades 3 through 7"--Provided by publisher.
  Includes bibliographical references and index.
  ISBN 978-1-60014-503-2 (hardcover : alk. paper)
  1. Near-death experiences--Juvenile literature. I. Title.
  BF1045.N4S76 2010
  133.901'3--dc22   2010011407

This edition first published in 2011 by Bellwether Media, Inc.

CONTENTS

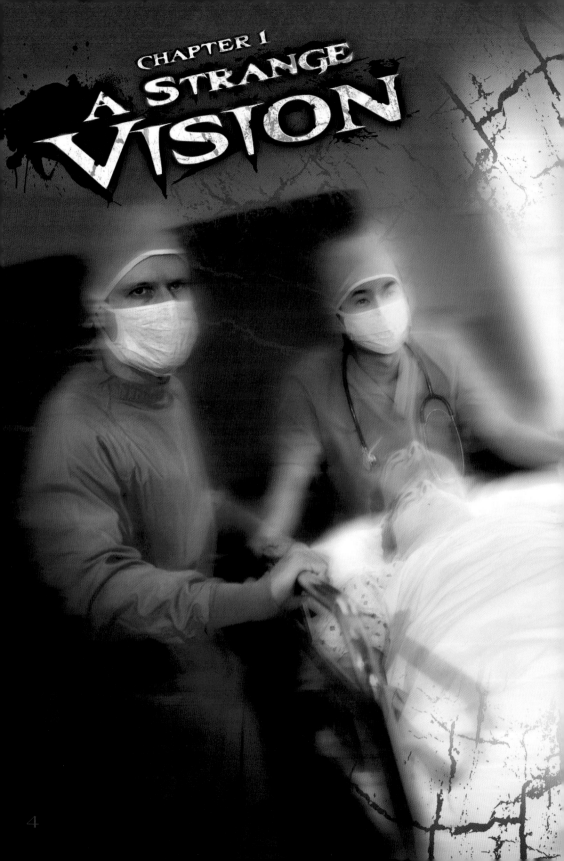

CHAPTER 1
A STRANGE VISION

On December 20, 1943, twenty-year-old George Ritchie died. At least that was what his doctors thought. After being dead for nine minutes, Ritchie shockingly came back to life. He never left his bed, but he claimed to have gone through an intense experience.

Ritchie said he remembered floating over his body. Then his life flashed before him. He saw his childhood and growth into an adult. He felt that he needed to do more in his life. He also claimed to see what he believed to be an **afterlife**. He was told he could not be part of it yet. Shortly after seeing it, he came back to life. Ritchie wrote a book about his experience. He later became a doctor and devoted his career to studying near-death experiences (NDEs).

Some people have claimed they had NDEs even when brain scans recorded no electrical activity. When they were revived, they reported near-death thoughts, feelings, and visions.

FLATLINED

CHAPTER 2
WHAT ARE NEAR-DEATH EXPERIENCES?

People have always wondered what will happen to them when they die. Is there something waiting for us after death? Many people report seeing visions when they are close to death. They sometimes hear and feel things too.

15 MILLION AND COUNTING

According to a Gallup poll from 1992, about 5 percent of Americans claim to have had an NDE. That is about 15 million people!

Many people describe floating over their bodies. This is called an **out-of-body experience**. Some people remember going through a long tunnel toward a light. Others have flashbacks. They see past events from their lives. People sometimes remember seeing or talking with loved ones who have died. Most people who claim to have had an NDE feel the need to live their lives differently. They say they have a new appreciation for life and a better understanding of death.

Skeptics say that there is a **biological** reason for NDEs. They argue that a lack of oxygen to the brain can result in dreamlike visions. They say that there is no reason to believe that NDEs are **supernatural**.

What causes NDEs? Does the human **consciousness** live on even after the brain dies, or is an NDE just the biological result of a dying brain? No one knows for sure.

KINDS OF NDEs

Name	
Tunnel Experience	
Life Review	
Beings of Light	
Out-of-Body Experience	
Peace and Well-Being	
Gift of Knowledge	
Conversation with Loved One	
Heavenly Message	
The Void	

Description

The sense of moving through a long tunnel, usually toward a source of warmth and light

The rapid review of one's entire life experience

Being surrounded by spirits full of light, sometimes the spirits of deceased loved ones

The sense of floating above one's body or of flying through the air without a body

Being filled with a sense of calm, peace, and well-being

Gaining a deeper understanding of life and death

The memory of speaking with a loved one, either alive or dead

Receiving a message from a supreme being; often the message is "It is not your time."

A feeling of emptiness, loneliness, or terrible dread

CHAPTER 3
SEARCHING FOR ANSWERS

Researchers have been studying NDEs for more than 100 years. Some researchers record statements from those who claim to have had NDEs. They look for common patterns. They try to figure out why so many people experience the same things. Some try to use NDEs to prove that an afterlife exists.

No. (# ___) | NAME Tosiane Antonette 1966

No. (# 247) | NAME David Oakford 1979
NOM

No. (# 19) | NAME George Ritchie
NOM

Others look for biological reasons for NDEs. They study chemicals in the brain. They look at how the brain works in its final moments. Some researchers think the brain enters a deep, dreamlike state. NDEs could be very similar to dreams. The brain may create these experiences to deal with the fear of death.

STAY OR GO?

Some people claim that in their near-death experiences, they were given a choice. They could go to an afterlife, or they could return to their bodies and living loved ones.

Many people want to believe that there is life after death. NDE reports give them hope. Do NDEs really give people a peek at an afterlife, or are they nothing more than the confused dreams of a dying brain? There is no way to prove either **theory**. The questions will likely remain a mystery forever.

GLOSSARY

afterlife—a form of spiritual existence after the death of the body

biological—having to do with natural bodily processes

consciousness—the mind's ability to recognize itself and its surroundings

out-of-body experience—an NDE in which a person floats outside of his or her body, often looking down on the body

skeptics—people who do not believe in something

supernatural—relating to existence in an unearthly realm

theory—an idea that tries to explain why something exists or happens

TO LEARN MORE

AT THE LIBRARY

Herbst, Judith. *Beyond the Grave*. Minneapolis, Minn.: Lerner Publications, 2005.

Martin, Michael. *Near-Death Experiences*. Mankato, Minn.: Capstone Press, 2005.

McCormick, Lisa Wade. *Near-Death Experiences: The Unsolved Mystery*. Mankato, Minn.: Capstone Press, 2009.

ON THE WEB

Learning more about near-death experiences is as easy as 1, 2, 3.

1. Go to www.factsurfer.com.

2. Enter "near-death experiences" into the search box.

3. Click the "Surf" button and you will see a list of related Web sites.

With factsurfer.com, finding more information is just a click away.

INDEX

The images in this book are reproduced through the courtesy of:
Mark Coffey, front cover, pp. 8-9; Tom Grill/Getty Images, pp. 4-5;
Paul Harizan/Getty Images, pp. 6-7; Oscar Burriel/Science Photo
Library, pp. 10-11; Jean-Claude Winkler/Getty Images, pp. 12-13;
Konstantin Chagin, pp. 16-17; Juan Martinez, pp. 18-19; Benjamin
Haas, pp. 20-21.